Handbook of
SHELLS

by
LULA SIEKMAN

Color Photos by
Richard van de Gohm

A Great Outdoors Book

Great Outdoors Publishing Company
An Imprint of Finney Company

ISBN 10: 0-8200-0208-9
ISBN 13: 978-0-8200-0208-8

Great Outdoors Publishing Company
An Imprint of Finney Company
8075 215th Street West
Lakeville, Minnesota 55044
www.floridabooks.com

Revised edition.

Printed in the United States of America

Interesting Facts About Shells

Seashells are divided into two classifications:
Univalves — Bivalves

Shells grow in all sizes, shapes and colors. All shells have life in them. Most of them grow by secreting a calcium carbonate from special glands located along the edge of the fleshy mantle of the animal.

To clean a shell; it should first be scrubbed with soap and water; the animal boiled and removed; then soaked in chlorine to whiten the shell or to remove the outer skin or periostracum.

Shells are found from shallow to deep water, under rocks, in mud, on seaweed, burrowed in corals or wood, in clean sand or on bushes, pilings or seawalls.

We get some of our best seafood from the shells, namely clams, oysters, and scallops.

Nearly all shells are found occasionally in a rare, pure white or albino form. They are not bleached or faded, but are pure white naturally.

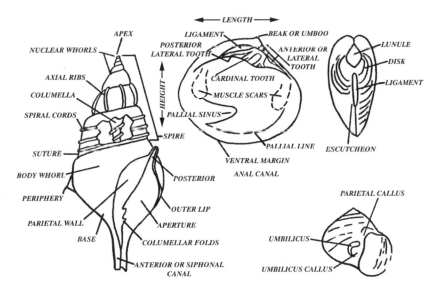

UNIVALVES

About 75% of all the shells are univalves, which means one shell, spiral in form. The animal in this shell is usually carnivorous and bores holes in other shells by means of a long tongue or radula which consists of many rows of very sharp teeth.

BIVALVES

The bivalve means two shells like a clam. These shells are joined together by a hinge. The bivalve gets its food by means of two tubes that constantly siphons water in through one tube and out the other. Most bivalves feed on algal cells and diatoms.

Top Shells

CAYENNE KEYHOLE LIMPET
Diodora cayenensis
Average size 1 inch, largest 2 inches; inedible.
Whitish-gray to dark gray. Inside white. Many
radial ribs with each fourth one larger. Deep pit just
behind the callus of the orifice on the inside.

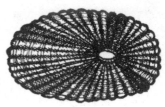

Often found attached to stones, or under stones.
Native to the Atlantic coast from New Jersey to Brazil.

FLORIDA TOP SHELL
Calliostoma euglyptum
Also called SCULPTURED TOP SHELL.
Average size ³/₄ inch, largest 1¹/₄ inches; inedible.
This shell is a rather dirty white splashed with
reds and browns, but it has a pearly lining. It is
pyramid shaped, sharply pointed at the apex, flat-
tened at the base. There are five or six whorls with
rounded shoulders decorated with rows of small
white "beads."
Found among seaweeds in rather shallow water and in water up to 32 fathoms.
Native from Cape Hatteras to Florida.

KNOBBY TOP
Turbo castanea
Also called CHESTNUT TURBAN.
Average size 1 inch high, largest 1¹/₂ inches; edible.
Usually light brown, blotched with darker brown;
occasionally dull green, gray or orange, with white
spots; interior pearly.

A solid, top-shaped shell with pointed apex.
Usually has five or six whorls decorated with bands of
bead-like structures—the latter more noticeable on the
shoulders. The outer lip is scalloped.
Found among seaweed and in shallow waters where there is grass.
Often used for ornamental purposes and in the making of jewelry.
Native from North Carolina to Florida, Texas and the West Indies.

Top and Star Shell

JUJUBE TOP
Calliostoma jujubinum

Average size ½ inch, largest 1¼ inches; inedible.

Buff background, mottled with gray and white streaks, some with reddish-brown. White iridescent interior.

Conical shape, with sharp pointed apex. There are eight to ten whorls; the lines between the whorls are not distinct. Fine-beaded ribs decorate the surface. The base is flattened. Has a deep, narrow, umbilicus (pit).

Found among seaweed in shallow water.

May be used in making jewelry or buttons.

Native to the west coast of Florida from Cedar Key to Cape Sable, the Bahamas and West Indies.

SMOOTH ATLANTIC TEGULA
Tegula fasciata

Average size ½ inch, largest ¾ inch; inedible.

Grayish-pink to yellow to brown, heavily marked with reds, browns or black. There may be a paler hand on the body-whorl.

The shell is a round pyramid with four or five whorls; it may be slightly concave just below dividing line. Surface is smooth, sometimes glossy, adults may have small teeth, pink inside lower margin. Opening oval.

Found among seaweed in shallow water or under rocks.

Used for necklaces, pearl ornaments and buttons.

Native to the waters of southern Florida and the West Indies

LONG-SPINED STAR-SHELL
Astraea phoebia

Average size 2 inches, largest 2½ inches; inedible.

White or dull brown on the outside. Interior white and polished.

A thin shell with long spines of imperfect shape. Turban shape with thick coils. Apex is flat and generally smooth. Shell has a heavy calcareous operculum.

Found on rocks.

Native to Florida Keys and West Indies.

Star and Tooth

IMBRICATE STAR-SHELL
Astraea tecta americana
Also called TUBED TURBAN SHELL.
Average size 1 inch in diameter, largest 1½ inches; inedible.

Grayish-white to dull green.
A solid and stony-looking shell with high apex.
Usually three whorls (can be seven or eight), with edges of having a scalloped appearance. Noticeable are the knobs at the shoulders. Five to eight delicate spiral cords at the base.

Usually found among seaweed in shallow water; often on algae-covered rocks.
Native to the Florida Keys and West Indies.

BLEEDING TOOTH
Nerita peloronta
Average size ¾ inch, largest 1½ inches; inedible.
Variable coloring, usually has streaks of purple on a white, pale orange or yellow background; outer lip is white as porcelain. Inside the opening a red area with 1 or 2 whitish teeth.

The outer lip is sharp edged, but thickened within. The toothed operculum fits perfectly in the shell opening.

Found on rocky shores facing open ocean.

One of the handsomest of nearly 200 similar shells, it is considered a valuable shell collection addition.

Native to Gulf waters, Key West to Bermuda, and the West Indies.

FOUR-TOOTHED NERITE
Nerita versicolor

Also called VARIEGATED NERITE. Average size ¾ inch, largest size 1 inch; inedible.

White in color with zigzag bands of black and red. Inside of shell white, but outer lip spotted with red and black. A thick, globe-shaped shell with almost no spire. It has numerous rounded ribs. The inside of the outer and inner lips each has several teeth.

Found on rocks at low tide.
Native from central Florida to the West Indies and Bermuda.

Periwinkle

ZICZAC PERIWINKLE
Littorina ziczac
Also called ZEBRA PERIWINKLE, ZIG-ZAG PERIWINKLE.
Average size 1 inch for female and ½ inch for male,
largest 2 inches; edible.

Dull white, with brownish, zigzag markings. A glob-
ular shell, turbinate like a snail. Females are higher than
they are wide, and smooth; the male is as high as it is wide with spiral grooves.

This mollusk lives attached to rocks above the tide line, or on mangrove roots
in Florida. Makes good fish bait, or food, if enough are captured to assemble for a
stew.

Native to the Florida Keys, Texas, West Indies and Bermuda.

MARSH PERIWINKLE
Littorina irrorata
Also called LINED PERIWINKLE.
Average size 1 inch, largest 2 inches; inedible.
Grayish-white with red-brown streaks on spiral
ridge, opening a yellow-white. Thick shell, cone-shaped.
The outer lip is sharp, strong, slightly flaring and yellowish
white.

Usually found in brackish water inlets, where it is often seen clinging to pilings,
roots, or grass stems. Has a habit of lying in the sun between tides.

Native to all coasts of the Gulf of Mexico. Sometimes found as far north as
Massachusetts.

ANGULATE PERIWINKLE
Littorina angulifera
Average size 1 inch, largest 1½ inches; edible.

Cream-colored overall, with dashes of reddish-purple,
although color varies from yellowish to orange or russet,
with darker splashes. Has a distinct pattern. Rather a thin
shell with a high spiral end and very thin outer lip.

Found almost entirely around estuaries, where inlets
of saltwater join freshwater. Is attached to any kind of wood immersed in the water. On pilings, it will be at the high tide line so that for many hours it is out of the water. Common on
trunks and branches of mangroves.

Native to all Florida waters from Jacksonville Beach around to Cedar Keys, especially in
the Florida Keys, and West Indies and Bermuda.

Sundial and Worm

SUNDIAL SHELL
Architectonica nobilis
Also called GRANULATED SUNDIAL SHELL, ARCHITECT'S SHELL, or COMMON SUNDIAL.

Average size 1 inch, largest 2 inches; inedible.

Lavender and white with tan spots on ridge next to suture.

Thick, flattened shell, circular in shape. The base is flat and decorated with many coiled, granulated ridges. The spiral whorls have furrows and ridges, and are segmented by dots and dashes that form a pattern resembling a sundial.

Found in sand below low water line.

Native from North Carolina to Florida, Texas and the West Indies.

FARGO'S WORMSNAIL
Vermicularia fargoi
Average size 1 inch, largest 3 inches; inedible.

Drab gray to yellowish-brown in color.

A rather thick, sturdy shell, the early whorls having two or three spiral cords, the rest of the whorls have thicker cords, brown-spotted. Thin threads run between the larger cords.

Found on mud flats.

Native from the west coast of Florida to Texas.

FLORIDA WORMSNAIL
Vermicularia knorri
Also called KNORR'S WORMSHELL, OLD MAID'S CURL.

Average size 4 inches, largest 8 inches; inedible.

Tip white and evenly coiled, with later spirals of yellowish or orange-brown.

The later coils are random with one or two spiral cords on each whorl. Thin threads are likely to be present, especially near the base.

Found in sponge masses. Often washed ashore.

Native from North Carolina to Florida and the Gulf of Mexico.

Worm, Button and Horn

WEST INDIAN WORMSNAIL
Vermicularia spirata
Average size 6 inches, largest 10 inches; inedible.

Amber, yellowish or an orange-brown.

A rather thin shell, the coils even and close for about ¼ inch, then drawn out and irregular. Early whorls smooth except for a spiral cord running across the middle of the whorl. Later whorls may have two cords, but not so well defined. Tiny threads sometimes visible, especially near base.

Found in shallow water, often in a tangled mass.

This shell is tightly coiled when young, but the adult shell is loosely coiled. It is tubelike, with coarse encircling growth lines, heavy longitudinal ribs and fine lines. The opening is round. The head has eyes, a toothed tongue and tentacles. May be found in groups, completely entangled, usually in shallow water, attached to stones or embedded in sponges or coral.

Most common on the Florida west coast from Tampa Bay south, and on the west coast from St. Augustine south to the West Indies.

BUTTONSNAIL
Modulus modulus
Average size ½ inch, largest ⅝ inch; inedible.

Light buff, with small dark spots and patches.

A very small shell, shaped like a "hammered down" snail. Has serrated edges along the opening.

Usually found in sand-mud bottoms of shallow bays.

Native from North Carolina to Texas, but particularly prevalent on the west coast of Florida.

DARK CERITH
Cerithium atratum

Also called FLORIDA HORN SHELL. Average size 1 inch, largest 1½ inches; inedible.

Whitish color with mottlings of tannish-brown.

Spiral rows of white "beads" with fine spiral lines in between. The shell is elongate with a sharp apex. The aperture is small and oblique, and there is a short anterior canal.

Found in moderately shallow water. Native from N. Carolina to South Florida.

Horn, Purple Snail and Staircase

FLY-SPECKED CERITHIUM
Cerithium muscarum
Also called DOTTED HORN SHELL.
Average size ³/₄ inch, largest size 1 inch; inedible.

The color is white or gray-white, with chestnut dots in spiral rows.
Elongated shell with acute apex. Nodules on whorls.
Common in shallow, warm waters.
Native to the south half of Florida and the West Indies.

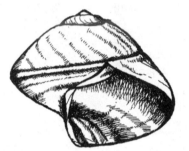

COMMON PURPLE SEA SNAIL
Janthina janthina
Also called VIOLET SNAIL.
Average size 1 inch, largest 1¹/₂; inedible.
Purplish-white on upper side, and darker purple on lower side.

The shell is thin and fragile. It has three or four sloping whorls. The opening is moderately large and oval-shaped. The outer lip is sharp. There is no umbilicus and no operculum. The spire is low. This shell is shaped much like the land snails.

Frail shell with a wavy outer lip. Whorls sloping and convex.

Animal lives some miles from land and only during a storm do the shells float ashore. It is carnivorous and secrete a purple fluid when disturbed.

Native to both coasts of Florida down to Vera Cruz, Mexico.

HUMPHREY'S WENTLETRAP
Epitonium humphreysii
Also called LADDER SHELL or STAIRCASE SHELL.
Average size, a little more than ¹/₂ inch, largest ³/₄ inch; inedible.

White in color. Usually has 9 or 10 convex whorls. Rather slender and thick. The surface is glossy. The lines dividing the whorls are deep, and the spire extended. The opening is almost circular, outer and lower part of lip somewhat flared.

These little shells inhabit the deep water generally, but may be found near shore.

Native from Cape Cod, Massachusetts to Florida and Texas.

Indian Boats or Slipper

ATLANTIC SLIPPER LIMPET
Crepidula fornicata

Also called BABY'S CRADLE, BOAT SHELL, SLIPPER
SHELL, or CANOE SHELL.

Average size 2 inches, largest 3 inches; edible.

White background with curved, chestnut-colored
stripes variously disposed. Inside is brown and shiny like
porcelain. A thin and translucent shell with an oval or
boat shape. There is a shelf or "seat" in the hinge end
which resembles the stem sheets on a boat.

These are usually found on muddy bottoms piled in groups of empty shells of
larger size. Quite plentiful on the Florida beaches. Often they attach themselves to
pen shells.

The animal can change sex, and it is interesting that in a large group, stacked
one atop the other, the top layers will be male, the bottom layers female, and a
section in the middle will be neuter, these were in the process of changing from
male to female. Gathered for curiosities, they make interesting additions to a shell
collection.

Native to all southern coasts from New Jersey to Texas.

SPOTTED SLIPPER LIMPET
Crepidula maculosa

Average size ½ inch, largest 1 inch; inedible,
White or cream color spotted with mauve or brown.
The edge of the lip is straight or only very slightly convex.
Strong but thin shell. Oval muscle scar.

Found attached to rocks, stones or other shells.

Native to west coast of Florida down to Vera Cruz, Mexico.

EASTERN WHITE SLIPPER LIMPET
Crepidula plana

Also called FLAT SHELL.

Average size ½ inch, largest 1½ inches; inedible.

White. This is one of the shells with a "seat" in the pointed end, however this one is quite flat, as distinguished from
the other Slipper Shells, which have round bottoms or "extended umbilicus."

Found in shallow water attached to large dead shells.

Native to all shores touched by the Gulf of Mexico, and from Canada to
Florida. Occasionally found in the West Indies.

Carrier and Conch

ATLANTIC CARRIER SNAIL
Xenophora conchyliophora
Average size 1½ inches (sans attachments), largest size 2 inches; inedible.

The shell is dirty white; the animal inside is bright red.

A circular shell, with deep impressions where the shell has attached other shells or stones to itself. From above it looks like a bunch of marine trash.

Found in deep warm waters.

Native from North Carolina to Key West and the West Indies.

QUEEN CONCH
Strombus gigas
Also called GIANT CONCH or PINK CONCH.
Average size 6 inches, largest 12 inches; edible.

Interior pink, yellow and highly polished; exterior rough and horny.

Very large. When full grown, weighs over 5 pounds. Has a large and pinkish lip with a brightly colored opening. The animal is quite powerful, using a foot to propel itself.

Found primarily in the coral reefs on the Florida Keys. A popular food among island people of the southern latitudes, this conch is considered an entertainment for the children, who listen to the sea roaring within, and valuable in the manufacturing of porcelain. Once piled by the hundreds in front of shell stands on Florida highways, they have now become endangered.

FLORIDA FIGHTING CONCH
Strombus alatus
Average size 3 inches, largest 4 inches; inedible.

Color is dark reddish-brown or orange-brown, and sometimes has zigzag bars of colors, on the body.

Shell has a heavy, expanded lip that is highly polished. It is usually spineless.

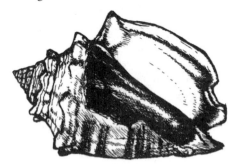

The animal is very active and progresses by a series of jumps, turning the shell from side to side. When placed on its back, it can somersault and right itself.

A very common shallow water species.

Native from the Carolinas to Florida.

Cowrie and Eye

MEASLED COWRIE
Cypraea zebra
Average size 2 inches, largest 5 inches; inedible.

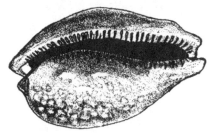

Light brown or yellowish-brown background, with large white spots over back; toward base, the spots have a brown center. Teeth dark brown, interior lavender.

A moderately thick shell, highly polished and quite smooth. The opening is toothed on both sides, extends the full length of the shell.

Much sought after by collectors for their individual beauty.

Native to the southern beaches of Florida, including the Florida Keys; also the West Indies.

SHARK EYE
Neverita duplicata
Also called DUPLICID MOONSNAIL or COMMON BULL'S EYE.

Average size 1 inch, largest 3 inches; inedible.

Slate-gray to tan, blending into white or creamy-white on base; interior chestnut colored. Umbilicus deep, but almost covered by a button-like brown callus.

A smooth and rounded shell, flatter than the usual Moon Shell, to which family it belongs.

Found on sand bars in shallow water.

Considered valuable to shell collections.

Native from Massachusetts to Florida and the Gulf states.

ATLANTIC DEER COWRIE
Macro cervus
Average size 3 inches, largest 7 inches; inedible.

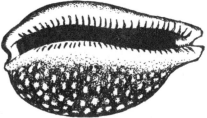

Small white spots on a dark brown background; base brown.

The shell is more inflated and larger than the Measled Cowrie. Animal has papillae on top of mantle. Seldom has ocellated spots on base.

Found under rocks near shore or on coral reefs.

Native from North Carolina to Florida and Cuba.

Moon, Bonnet and Fig

COLORFUL MOONSNAIL
Natica canrena
Also called COLORFUL ATLANTIC NATICA.
Average size 1 inch, largest 2 inches; inedible.

Whitish background is streaked with spiral chestnut
and purple bands, with a zigzag or wavy appearance.
Interior is light chestnut, fading to white at the lip.

A heavy and smooth shell, looking much like a snail. Has a large opening, considering the overall size of the shell. Found on intertidal sand flats.

Native from North Carolina to Florida and the West Indies.

SCOTCH BONNET
Semicassis granulata granulata
Average size 1½ inches, largest 3 inches; inedible.

Creamy-white background with tannish-brown rectangles in circular rows.

Low spire with about 20 spiral grooves on the large body whorl.
Outer lip thickened. Sometimes the shell appears beaded by the weak axial ribs.

Parietal wall extends out over the large body whorl in a small shield. The siphonal canal is short and recurved. The outer lip is strongly toothed.

Found in shallow water and commonly washed ashore.

Native from North Carolina to Gulf of Mexico and the West Indies.

ATLANTIC FIG SHELL
Ficus communis
Also called PAPER FIG SHELL,
COMMON FIG SHELL.

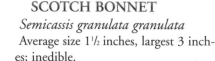

Average size 3 inches, largest 4 inches; inedible.

Light brown, with a lining of deeper brown

A very thin, pear-shaped shell, finely ribbed. Very light in weight. Fragile, with low spire and large aperture.

These are the light and delicate shells often found high on the beaches. Being lighter than all the others, they usually take the top of the heap in the shell windrows of shell beaches; otherwise found in deep water.

Native from North Carolina south to all Florida coasts and the Bahamas.

Murex Shells

APPLE MUREX
Chicoreus pomum

Average size 2 to 3 inches, largest 4½ inches; inedible.

Yellowish-white, with broad stripes and brown mottling, the opening tinted with pink, yellow or orange, with a brown spot inside.

A heavy, rough shell with a well-developed spire and a large body-whorl. There are three prominent vertical ridges on each whorl and the surface is modular; also has fine, cord-like ribs, The opening is large and circular. Outer lip is thickened, and scalloped with 3 or 4 brown spots. Canal is short and curved backward from the opening.

Prefers rocky or gravelly bottom and moderately shallow water; feeds on dead crabs or fish. Empty shells may be found on the beaches.

Native from North Carolina to Florida and West Indies.

LACE MUREX
Chicoreus florifer dilectus

Average size 1 to 2 inches, largest 3 inches; inedible.

A deep brownish-black, light brown, or whitish, with a pink apex and opening. Young shells, and some well-worn adults, may be pink all over.

A sturdy, rather elaborate shell with about seven whorls. There are rounded, revolving cords crossed by three prominent ribs. The shell is decorated with spines which are most striking near the outer lip. The canal, flattened below, is curved backward. The opening is small and round.

Prefers sandy bottoms in fairly deep water, also found among mangroves or muddy uses or rocks.

Native to southern Florida and the Keys, and the West Indies.

WHITE BABY EAR
Sinum perspectivum

Also called EAR SHELL, BABY'S EAR MOONSNAIL.

Average size 1 inch, largest 2 inches; inedible.

Pure white with a yellowish skin.

Thick, smooth shell a bit wider than it is high. Somewhat resembling an ear. The animal envelopes the shell.

An oyster eater usually found on broken shell bottom and shallow sandy areas.

Native to Virginia and down to Florida coasts and the West Indies. Most common on the west coast of Florida.

Oyster Drills

THICK-LIP DRILL
Eupleura caudata
Also called RIBBED OYSTER DRILL.
Average size ¹/₂ inch, largest 1 inch;,
inedible.
Usually brown, overlaid with dull white.
The ribs are pure white.

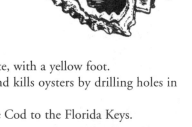

The shell is small and quite strong, with
about five whorls sharply angled with spiral
cords and prominent ribs. The animal is white, with a yellow foot.
Found on oyster beds, where it attacks and kills oysters by drilling holes in
the shells.
Native to the Atlantic coast south of Cape Cod to the Florida Keys.

SHARP-RIBBED DRILL
Eupleura sulcidentata
Average size ¹/₂ inch, largest size 1 inch;
inedible.
Color is gray, brown, tan and sometimes
pinkish

High spire. Long canal. Thickened lip. The axial ribs are sometimes sharp.
There are 2 or 3 axial ribs between the two large varices.
Found among the rocks at low tide.
Native to west coast of Florida

ATLANTIC OYSTER DRILL
Urosalpinx cinerea
Average size ¹/₂ inch, largest 1 inch; inedible.
Grayish, dull white, sometimes yellow or
light brown spirals. Opening is brown.

Shell is small, thin and rough with a high
spire. There are fine revolving longitudinal ribs. Outer lip slightly thick on inside.
The male shells are smaller than the female shells, The female spawns once a year
and lays about 25 to 28 leathery, vase-shaped capsules, each containing 8 to 12
eggs. These shells can be found from intertidal areas down to 25 feet, but they
move inshore to spawn. Found near oyster beds. A vicious enemy to oysters. Has
the ability to bore a hole and suck out the oyster.
Native from Nova Scotia to Southern Florida Introduced to U.S. west coast
and northern Europe.

Dog Whelk, Dove and Cantharus

BRUISED NASSA
Nassarius vibe

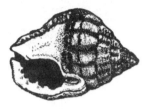

Also called MOTTLED DOG WHELK, COMMON EAST-
ERN NASSA. Average size ½ inch, largest ¾ inch; edible.

Gray-brown to white in color, marked with
reddish-brown. May show different color patterns
indifferent localities. Dead shells tend to lose color.
Inside opening is sometimes yellowish.

A short, heavy shell with about five whorls, the dividing lines well defined. There
are strong longitudinal folds and less definite circular lines. The opening is notched
top and bottom, the outer tip thick, the inner with a heavy patch of enamel.

Abundant in sandy bays and quiet water.

Native from North Carolina to Florida, the Gulf states and West Indies. More
plentiful on Florida shores than in north.

GREEDY DOVE-SNAIL
Costo avara

Also called AVARA DOVE SHELL. Average size, just
under ½ inch, largest just under 1 inch; inedible.
Brownish-yellow in color.

A thick, strong shell with a tall-pointed spire. There are six to seven whorls
with spiral lines and vertical folds. The body whorl has about twelve of these folds,
not going below the middle of the shell; beneath the folds there are only the spiral
lines. The outer lip is slightly toothed within.

Lives below the low-tide level on the beaches.

Native to the east and west coast of Florida, it
may be found as far north as Cape Cod and
south to the West Indies.

TINTED CANTHARUS
Pollia tincta

Also called MOTTLED SPINDLE.

Average size ¾ inch, largest size 1¼ inches; inedible.

Variegated pattern of yellow, orange, lavender and grayish-brown.

Shell ovate, thick, with spire evenly conic. Aperture oval, with canal at both top
and bottom. Axial ribs low and weak. Spiral cords numerous and weak. Inside of
outer lip with small teeth which are strongest near the top.

Found in shallow water. The young are easily confused with members of the
Thais family.

Native from North Carolina to both sides of Florida, Texas and the West Indies.

King's Crown and Whelk

CROWN CONCH
Melongena corona
Also called KING'S CROWN.
Average size 2 inches, largest 4 inches; edible.

White background and wavy hands of brown; the interior is milky-white.

The name "King's Crown" comes from the row of spines on the apex which gives the appearance of a crown.

An aggressive mollusk. It can drill holes in either bivalves or univalves. It is most often found in mucky mud, frequently on oyster beds in shallow water where it feeds on either dead or live animals.

Native to Florida, the Gulf States and Mexico.

LIGHTNING WHELK
Busycon sinistrum
Also called LEFT-HANDED WHELK.
Average size 4 inches, largest 16 inches; edible.

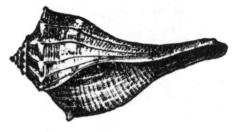

Gray-white in color, with uneven streaks of purple-brown.

Small knobs, triangular in shape, rise from the shoulder. It is a light shell with a short spine, long canal and aperture.

Found in subtropical waters on mud flats and in grass.

Native from South Carolina to Texas—common on the west coast of Florida and in the Gulf States.

PEAR WHELK
Busycotypus spiratus
Average size 3 inches, largest 4 inches; edible.

Creamy-white, with yellowish-brown lines on body-whorl.

Shell is somewhat pear-shaped with a short spire. It has smooth, rounded shoulders.

Aperture large with long canal, thin lip.

Found in shallow, sandy, clear water.

Native from North Carolina to the Gulf States.

Tulip and Horse Conch

TRUE TULIP
Fasciolaria tulipa
Average size 2 inches, largest 8 inches; inedible.

Color pinkish-gray to reddish-brown, sometimes almost black, with white blotches or streaks.

Shell spindle-shaped with a moderately high spire. Shell has revolving lines that are crinkled on the body whorl. Aperture long and oval, operculum horny and siphonal canal open and white.

Found in shallow water in grassy flats.

Native from North Carolina to Florida, Texas said West Indies.

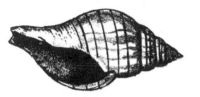

EASTERN BANDED TULIP
Fasciolaria hunteria
Also called PALE TULIP.
Average size 2 inches, largest 4 inches; inedible.

Pearly-gray, with delicate lines in dark brown or black banding the shell in parallel lines. Smooth surface. Moderately high spire, five or six whorls, aperture egg-shaped with short, wide canal.

Usually found in mud flats, and just below the surface of the bottom.

Native to Texas, Louisiana and Alabama,

HORSE CONCH
Pleuroploca gigantea
Also called GIANT BAND SHELL.

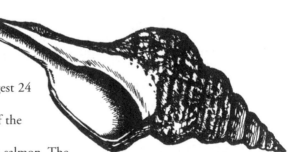

Average size 12 inches, largest 24 inches; edible.

This is one of the largest of the Florida shells.

Exterior white or brownish-salmon. The inside of the lip is tannish-orange. The shell is rather solid, with the spire elevated and sharply pointed. One of the distinguishing features is that this species has giant nodules; in other, similar species they are much less prominent or lacking.

Found in shallow water on grassy flats.

Native from North Carolina to Florida.

Vase, Panama and Rice

CARIBBEAN VASE SHELL
Vasum muricatum
Also called SPINY VASUM.
Average size 2½ inches, largest 4 inches; inedible.

White, or white with brown, irregular longitudinal lines on the body whorl. Interior white, with brown markings.

A solid shell, thick and triangular in shape, usually having three rows of blunt spines and with coarse spiral ridges around the body whorl.

Found in clear ocean or gulf waters.

Native to the Florida Keys and the West Indies.

LETTERED OLIVE
Oliva sayana
Also called PANAMA SHELL.
Average size 2 inches, largest 2½ inches; inedible.

Light brown coloring with an overlay of darker brown which resembles lettering. It has a glossy finish.

This mollusk is most always found alive, and can be located by the burrowing ridge it makes in the sand at low tide which somewhat resembles a mole in a field of farm land. These mollusks usually live in colonies.

The shells have a beautiful polished appearance when cleaned properly. A good method is to bury them in sand for several weeks and the ants will eat the animal. A good rinsing in sea water completes the operation.

Native from North Carolina to the Gulf Coast, particularly the Florida Gulf Coast. The largest colonies are located about Sarasota Bay and near the Gulf passes.

RICE OLIVE
Olivella floralia

Also called COMMON RICE SHELL. Average size ³⁄₈ inch, largest ½ inch; inedible.

All white, with the apex sometime white, purplish or orange. Small folds on the columella. High spire, four whorls, aperture long and narrow with a thin, sharp lip.

Members of the Olivella family have an operculum. Members of the Oliva family do not.

Common in shallow water. Native from North Carolina to Florida and the West Indies.

Junonia, Nutmeg and Marginella

JUNONIA
Scaphella junonia

Average size 3 inches, largest 4 inches; inedible.

Creamy white, marked with spiral rows of brown or orange spots with a squarish shape. Has a porcelain white lining.

Shaped like a slim, delicate spindle with a thin lip.

This is a true deep-sea mollusk, found on the beaches of shelling islands after a storm, particularly Sanibel Island on the Florida West Coast. Best specimens are found completely covered with sand.

This rare shell is considered a precious find to collectors.

Native from North Carolina to Florida and Texas.

COMMON NUTMEG
Cancellaria reticulata

Also called CROSS-BARRED SHELL.

Average size 1 inch long, largest 1³/₄ inches; edible.

Background of white, with various shades of brown markings arranged in spiral bands and longitudinal stripes.

Shell resembles a nutmeg in shape, with the same roughness of texture. It is heavy and spherical, with both ends pointed.

Mostly seen in grassy bottoms or kelp beds, it is vegetarian.

Native to the Florida West Coast, mostly around Cape Sable and as far north as North Carolina.

COMMON ATLANTIC MARGINELLA
Prunum apicinum

Average size ¹/₂ inch, largest; ³/₄ inch; inedible.

Usually ivory-white to yellow, with two or three pale brown bands, with two red-brown dots near the middle and a smaller one at the bottom and at the top.

Solid and highly polished, with the a rather flat spire and a large body-whorl. Opening is long and narrow, nearly the length of the shell. The shell has a rather thick outer lip and four distinct folds on the inner.

Found in sandy places in bays and shallow waters.

Native to Florida beaches, but may be found as far north as the Carolinas, and as far south as the West Indies.

Cone Shells

ALPHABET CONE
Conus spurius
Average size 2 inches, largest 3 inches; inedible.
A smooth white shell with rows of "characters" in brown and orange, arranged in more or less regular spiral bands. Interior white. Thin, brown outer skin.

Cone-shaped with flat top. The opening is long and narrow.

About ten whorls, with the first five whorls being flat and the last five whorls revolving to a high apex. Outer lip moderately thin and slightly curved in an elongated semi-circle.

May be found on sand bars and grassy flats of inland waters.

Native from North Carolina to Florida

FLORIDA CONE
Conus floridanus
Average size 1½ inches, largest 2 inches; inedible.

Color is variable from white to buff with spots of yellow, tan and sometimes orange-brown. Moderately high spire with 7 or 8 whorls. There is usually a white band around the middle of the large whorl.

This is a moderately heavy shell. The aperture, or opening, is long and narrow. The outer lip is thin and sharp. Many of the cone shells show injuries consisting of a long uneven line that has healed and then gone on to grew a new outer lip./

Conus floridanus floridensis is a dark color form with spiral rows of reddish-brown dots.

Found on sand flats, in rock crevices or under stones.

Native to North Carolina and Florida.

JASPER CONE
Conus jaspideus
Average size ½ inch, largest ¾ inch; inedible.
Dull grayish color with reddish-brown mottlings.

High spire with strong spiral lines cut into the sides, usually right up to the shoulder. The aperture is long and narrow with a thin outer lip. There are eight whorls leading to the apex with the sutures being distinct between each whorl.

Common to shallow sandy water.

Native to south half of Florida and West Indies.

Cone, Auger and Bubble

CROWN CONE
Conus regius
Also called CLOUDY CLONE.
Average size 2 inches, largest 3 inches; inedible.
Generally a mottled chocolate-brown and white

porcelain-like shell, although the color may vary,
even within the same locality. A rare yellow form may be
found occasionally. Interior white. The surface is sculptured with spiral threads or
bead-like structures, especially pronounced on the low spire. It has from five to
eight whorls and a long, narrow opening that is finely toothed along the inner
margin of the lip.

Found among reefs and rocky bottoms.

Native from southern Florida to Cuba and the Antilles. Uncommon in Florida.

EASTERN AUGER
Terebra dislocata
Also called DISLOCATED TEREBRA, DISLO-
CATED AUGER, or COMMON ATLANTIC AUGER.
Average size 1 inch, largest 2 inches; inedible.

Sometimes grayish and sometimes yellowish-brown in color. Usually mottled
one color on the other. A long and tapering shell with many whorls. There is a
beaded band on the whorl of this species.

The exterior surface of the shell is decorated with fine spiral grooves and wavy
longitudinal folds. The aperture is small and the operculum is yellow and horny.
Just under the suture is the knobby spiral band, which gives the shell the appearance of being composed of alternating large and small whorls.

Native from Virginia to Florida, Texas and the West Indies.

COMMON WEST INDIAN BUBBLE
Bulla striata
Average size ¹/₂ inch, largest 1 inch; inedible.
Color varies from whitish with mottlings or
bands of brown, to a pale red with purple-brown.

An oval shell, smooth and inflated, the spire
depressed. Opening is longer than the shell and
rounded at both ends. Many fine lines mark the surface.

Found at low tide on grassy mud flats. Most easily obtained at night.

Native from North Carolina to Florida and West Indies.

Chiton, Tooth and Nautilus

COMMON WEST INDIAN CHITON
Chiton tuberculatus

Also called COAT-OF-MAIL.
Average size 2 inches, largest 3 inches; inedible.
Grayish to greenish-brown.
Oblong, with 8 overlapping plates, one of which is pictured here. Chitons in Florida are small and inconspicuous. They curl up when taken from the rocks or shells.
Native to Florida, Texas, and the West Indies.

AMERICAN TUSKSHELL
Dentalium laqueatum

Also called PLOW-FOOTED SHELL, PANELLED TOOTH SHELL, WAMPUM, or PAN-ELLED TUSK.
Average size 1 inch, largest 2½ inches; inedible.
Color is solid white. A cylindrical shell, open at both ends, resembling the tusk of an animal.
This member of the tooth shell family of tooth shells has a long history of collection. The ancient Indians and Alaskan tribes used this shell as money.
Native from North Carolina to South Florida and the West Indies.

GREATER ARGONAUT
Argonauta argo

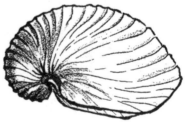

Also called PAPER NAUTILUS.
Average size 4 inches, largest 8 inches; inedible.
Thin and flat, spiral at one end and semi-circular in shape, decorated with small knobs and veins.
This shell is an egg case used by the female to contain her eggs. Since she is provided with eight arms, as the eggs grow larger (they look like tiny bunches of grapes), the nautilus, pushed from the shell, grasps it in her arms and floats to the surface. There the eggs hatch and the young swim away.
Found in tropical waters, on the floor of the ocean. They come to the surface in summer at breeding time.
Prized among collectors. Sailors believe them a sign of fair wind and good weather.
Native to the Florida coast and in most tropical waters.

Turkey Wing and Ark

TURKEY WING
Arca zebra

Average size 2 inches, largest 3 inches; edible.

White background with brown markings, in zigzag pattern.

Interior tinged with lavender, with deeper lavender bordering margin.

Surface of shell gives appearance of being sculptured, with strong radial ribs and thread-like markings. Has a long, narrow hinge line with numerous small teeth.

Found attached to rocks by its byssus.

Used widely for making shell novelties.

Native to the east and west coasts of Florida, also from North Carolina to Bermuda.

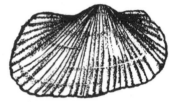

TRANSVERSE ARK
Anadara transversa

Average size ³/₄ inch, largest 1¹/₄ inches; inedible.

White inside and outside.

Box-shaped, with left valve overlapping right valve. Ligament fairly long. Ribs on left valve usually beaded, but right valve rarely so; 30 to 35 ribs per valve. Periostracum brownish-gray.

Fairly common in mud, below water line.

Native from Cape Cod to Florida and Texas.

MOSSY ARK
Arca imbricata

Also called NOAH'S ARK.

Average size 1¹/₂ inches, largest 2¹/₂ inches; edible.

Color brownish. The outer skin is quite heavy and brown. Shell is purplish-white inside and out.

The shell is rather elongated. The front end is round and the back is shaped like the keel of a ship. It has four or five beaded ribs. The rest of the surface is cross-ribbed with growth lines. It has red blood and a fringe of eyes on the mantle's edge.

Found under rocks in shallow water. It may also be found as a fossil in beds south of Lake Okeechobee.

Native from North Carolina to the West Indies.

Ark, Mussel and Oyster

PONDEROUS ARK
Noetia ponderosa
Average size 2 inches, largest 2½ inches; edible.

A white shell with black skin. Viewed from the end, it is heart-shaped, thick, box-like and ribbed. The ribs are raised and square, split down the center by an engraved line.

Found in shallow water. A sand dweller.

Native from Virginia to Key West, Louisiana and the Gulf of Mexico, it is found more abundantly in the south.

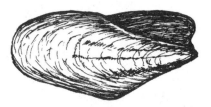

AMERICAN HORSEMUSSEL
Modiolus americanus
Average size 1 inch, largest 4 inches; inedible.

Outside yellowish-brown periostracum, underneath, a rose color. Sometimes streaked with light purple. Interior dull white stained rose, bluish or brownish.

The surface is smooth with a shiny periostracum. The anterior end if short and narrow, the posterior end broadly rounded. The shell is thin and moderately high.

Found rather commonly on our southern shores. Sometimes found attached to Gorgonias or commonly washed ashore in clusters.

Native from North Carolina to the West Indies.

ATLANTIC WING-OYSTER
Pteria colymbus
Average size 1½ inches, largest 3 inches; edible.

Outside color can be brown, black or brown-purple with broken lines of cream or white. Interior pearly with a margin of purplish-black with the cream rays showing through.

Fairly thin-shelled. It is obliquely oval with a tong extension of the hinge line toward the posterior end. Has a strong anterior notch for the byssus. Sometimes found attached to Gorgonia.

Common from low water to several fathoms.

Native from North Carolina to Florida and the West Indies.

Oyster and Penshell

ATLANTIC PEARL-OYSTER
Pinctada imbricata
Also called the PEARLY OYSTER.
Average size 1½ inches, largest 3 inches; edible.
The color varies from brown to green, mottled
with purplish-brown or black. The inside is pearly
with a brown border.

A flat, squarish shell, usually with scaly projections arranged concentrically.
Found in deep water, it is often brought in by
sponge fishermen, and is found in shallow water attached to rocks.
Native from South Carolina to Florida, to Texas and West Indies.

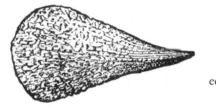

SAWTOOTH PENSHELL
Atrina serrata
Also called HALF-NAKED PEN SHELL.
Average size 6 inches, largest 10 inches;
edible.
Brownish and scaly, with iridescent lining.
Hinge is straight and outside edge curved.
Thin and fragile. Has a smoky appearance and horny texture. At the pointed end
the scales are very thin.
Native from North Carolina to Florida, to Texas and West Indies.

STIFF PEN SHELL
Atrina rigida
Average size 5 inches, largest 9
inches; edible.
Dull reddish-brown; interior pearly and
iridescent. A triangular-shaped shell with the hinge
side straight and opposite side curved. Has a horny texture
with erect, prickly spines.
An abundant shell on Florida's west coast, sometimes found attached to mangrove roots, often on the beaches.
Native from North Carolina to the Caribbean and the Gulf of Mexico.

Cat's Paw and Scallop

ATLANTIC KITTENPAW
Plicatula gibbosa

Also called CAT'S PAW.

Average size ¹/₂ inch, largest 1 inch; inedible.

Dirty white to gray, with brownish-red or purplish lines on the ribs.

Shell strong and cat's paw shaped, with heavy ribs numbering 5 to 7, which give the valves a wavy, interlocking margin.

Found in piles of shells along the intertidal lines. Fairly common.

Native from North Carolina to Florida and the Gulf states and the West Indies.

ORNATE SCALLOP
Chlamys ornata

Average size 1 inch, largest 1¹/₂ inch; edible.

White, spotted with red and purple.

About twenty ribs, a few generally unspotted. The ribs have sharp scales, especially near margins. The wings are unequal in size, one being scarcely noticeable. Beach-worn shells have usually lost their scales.

Found in shallow water among the seaweed.

These fragile little shells are used extensively in making shell jewelry.

Native to southern Florida to the West Indies.

BAY SCALLOP
Argopecten irradians concentricus

Average size 2 inches, largest 3 inches; edible.

Lower valve is commonly all white or is lightest in color. The upper valve is brown or bluish gray.

Has 19 to 21 squarish ribs. Lower valve is fatter than the upper valve.

Found in shallow waters, it is a sought-after edible mollusk.

Native from Virginia, Georgia, Louisiana to Tampa, Florida.

The subspecies *Argopecten irradians amplicostatus* has only 12 to 17 ribs. The lower valve is commonly white while the upper valve is dark. It has high, squarish ribs that are slightly rounded. It is more gibbose than *A. i. concentricus*.

Ranges from central Texas to Mexico

Scallop or Pectin Shell

ZIGZAG SCALLOP
Euvola ziczac

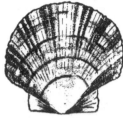

Also called FAN SHELL.

Average size 2 inches in diameter, largest 3 inches; edible.

A pinkish-violet shade at apex with reddish-brown stripes radiating out. Circular markings are usually yellow or pale pink.

A shell much like shallow-water scallops, only living in deeper water, usually 30 feet deep. Often found cast on the beaches when the animal has been killed.

Native to Florida west coast waters on the Gulf of Mexico and from North Carolina to the West Indies.

ATLANTIC CALICO SCALLOP
Argopecten gibbus

Average size 1 inch, largest 2 inches; inedible.

Found in many colors, usually with bright orange, lavender, purple, brown with white rays and white with purple markings. Rarest color is lemon-yellow; 19 to 21 ribs. Wings about equal in size.

A favorite with shell collectors, who strive to get the greatest variety of shadings. Some collectors have a hundred calicos, all of different color combinations.

Native from the coast of North Carolina to the Gulf of Mexico and the West Indies.

LION'S PAW
Lyropecten nodosus

Also called KNOBBY SCALLOP.

Average size 3 inches, largest 4 inches; edible.

Deep red or dark orange.

This is a scallop-shaped shell, but does look something like a spread-out paw of a lion, when you study it. There are heavy ribs and wide spaces between. The knobs along the ribs further identify it. Also the ears are not of equal size. Because it has a strong hinge, perfect pairs are often found. Considered on the rare side. Usually only found after a hard northwest blow.

Native to the Florida coasts.

Jingle and Oyster

COMMON JINGLE
Anomia simplex

Also called BABY'S FOOT SHELL or SMOOTH JINGLE SHELL.
Average size ¹/₂ inch, largest 2 inches; edible (but not popular).

Translucent. Solid coloring—orange, yellow, salmon-pink, white, slate-gray or jet black.

The shape is irregular, usually determined by the object to which it is attached. There is an odd scar inside the shell near the valves that resembles a baby's footprint.

The name "jingle shell" is derived from the fact that a handful of them makes a pleasant jingling sound when shaken.

Found on both coasts of Florida in great numbers. Sometimes beaches are piled high with them. They are often attached to submerged objects, so thickly that one grows on top of another, Oyster dredges bring them in quantity.

Native from Massachusetts to Florida, to Texas and the West Indies.

FROND OYSTER
Dendostrea frons

Also called COON OYSTER. Average size 1 inch, largest 2 inches; edible, but small.

Interior translucent white, exterior white and purplish-red.

Beaks curved; often elongated and attached to stem of trees by a series of clasping projections of the shell, but the shell may be oval in design according to the object it has attached itself to.

Found on mangrove trees or attached to rocks and stationary objects. Raccoons love them. They are too small for marketing commercially.

Native to Florida, the Gulf Coast and the West Indies.

LEAFY JEWELBOX
Chama macerophylla

Also called LEAFY ROCK OYSTER.
Average size 1 inch, largest 3 inches; edible.

A variety of colors from violet to a lavender-pink or lemon-yellow.

Both valves have lace-like, ruffled edges and an irregular shape.

Found in shallow water.

Native from North Carolina to all Florida coasts and the West Indies.

Oysters and Cardita

FLORIDA SPINY JEWELBOX
Arcinella cornuta
Average size 1 inch, largest 1½ inches; edible.
White or ivory-white in color. Inside white or
tinted with orchid.
Rectangular in shape, this is a heavy, rather
inflated shell. From seven to nine rows of long,
thick spines.
Found in warm seas from 3 to 40 fathoms. Often
washed ashore.
Native from North Carolina to Florida and Texas.

EASTERN OYSTER
Crassostrea virginica
Also called VIRGINIA OYSTER.
Average size 2 inches, largest 6 inches; edible.
Dirty-gray exterior; white inside with a purple scar.
This is the familiar oyster which varies greatly in size
and shape. The margins are only slightly undulating or
straight. The beaks are usually long and strongly curved. A
heavy shell.

Eggs are small, produced in large numbers at one
spawning (about 50 million) and are fertilized and develop in the open water outside of the parent. They smother in mud, so oyster fishermen throw back millions
of pounds of oyster shell for the tiny oysters to attach themselves to in the quiet
waters of bays and inlets.
Native from Gulf of St. Lawrence to the Gulf of Mexico and the West Indies.

BROAD-RIBBED CARDITID
Carditamera floridana
Also called BIRD WING SHELL.
Average size 1 inch, largest 1½ inches; inedible.
Exterior is white with purple or chestnut
blotches. Interior is white.
This shell is small, thick, radially ribbed and
has a byssus. Surface has 20 strong raised, beaded,
radial ribs. Beaks close together.
This is a common shell that is washed ashore on the Florida beaches. Used in
making jewelry.
Native to Florida and Mexico.

Lucine

MANY-LINE LUCINE
Parvilucina crenella
Average size ¼ inch, largest ⅜ inch; inedible.
White, both interior and exterior.
Moderately thick-shelled, round and obese. Radial ribs and concentric lines. Inner margin very finely denticulate. The irregular, concentric hump in the shell is caused by growth after a long rest.

Common from shoreline to 120 fathoms.
Native from North Carolina to both coasts of Florida.

FLORIDA LUCINE
Pseudomiltha floridana
Average size 1 inch, largest 1½ inches; inedible.
White, with a dirty-white periostracum.
Shell round and strong. Hinge plate fairly wide and strong, with the teeth barely defined. Smooth except for a few weak growth lines. Found in moderately shallow water. The beaks turn forward and are small, but prominent. This shell may be distinguished from the other members of the family by its rather indistinct posterior fold and the fact that it is not as thick.
Some shell shops called these "face shells," because they were used for the faces of shell dolls.
Ranges from the west coast of Florida to Texas.

PENNSYLVANIA LUCINE
Lucina pennsylvanica
Average size 1 inch, largest 2 inches; inedible.
Pure white with a yellow periostracum.
Concentric ridges distinct and delicate. Beach-worn specimens are smooth and shiny. Lunule heart-shaped.
A small and extremely thick shell distinguished by a diagonal furrow about the posterior region. Ovate and inflated. The beak is inclined forward. There are widely-separated, sharp, concentric ridges on the outer surface.
Found in shallow water.
Native from North Carolina to the Florida east coast and the West Indies.

Buttercup, Lucina and Cockle

BUTTERCUP LUCINE
Anodontia alba

Also called APRICOT SHELL.
Average size 1½ inches, largest 2 inches; inedible.
White outside, inside butter-colored or yellowish-orange. Another species, *Anodontia philippiana,* is chalky white with no orange color in interior.

A very beautiful and delicate bowl-shaped shell, with the characteristic that both valves are of equal size. Seldom are both halves of the shell found, since the hinge is very weak.

This deep-water mollusk reaches the beach when tidal flow washes it up. Native from North Carolina to Florida, to the Gulf states and the West Indies.

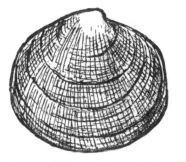

DWARF TIGER LUCINE
Codakia orbiculata

Average size 2½ inches, largest 3 inches; inedible.

Pure white, tinged with yellow or red-violet around edges.

A large shell, fairly thick. Ridges radiating from the beak are crossed by fine, concentric lines.

Usually found on sandy bottoms. The largest of the species in southern waters.

Native to all coasts of Florida and West Indies.

YELLOW PRICKLYCOCKLE
Trachycardium muricatum

Average size 2 inches in height, largest size 2½ inches; edible.

Outside of shell light cream or yellowish, with splotches of reddish-brown.

Inside white, tinted with yellow.

Thick, oval, with 30 to 40 moderately-scaled, radiating ribs. Margins deeply crenulated. A common shallow water species.

Native from North Carolina to West Indies and Texas.

Cockle

FLORIDA PRICKLYCOCKLE
Trachycardium egmontianum
Also called ROSE COCKLE.
Average size 1 inch in height, largest 2 inches; edible.
Outside white with splotches of reddish-brown and tan. Inside white with splotches of orange, reddish-purple or salmon.
Shell is thick and more elongate than oval, as in the yellow cockle. Has 27 to 31 strong, prickly, radial ribs.
A common shallow-water species, especially on the Gulf side.
Native from South Carolina to Florida and the West Indies.

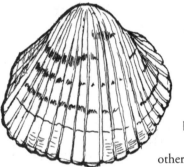

GIANT ATLANTIC COCKLE
Dinocardium hyningi
Also called, VAN HYNING'S COCKLE or LARGE BROWN COCKLE. Average size 3 inches, largest 4 inches; edible.
Color pattern is buff, yellowish-brown and reddish-brown in irregular bands. Interior lighter brown, with a white band around the margin.
A large thick shell. Has greater dimensions than others of the family, sometimes as much as 5 inches across. The living mollusk is well equipped with strong muscles. The largest of the species.
Native to the Florida west coast beaches from Clearwater south to Cape Sable.

EGG COCKLE
Laevicardium laevigatum
Also called BUTTER SHELL or COMMON EGG COCKLE.
Average size 1 inch, largest 2 inches; inedible.
Cream color, tinged with yellow, with concentric markings of light brown. Interior is polished white, sometimes pinkish-tinged.
This shell is smooth and shiny, and those on the east coast have the appearance of being lacquered. Unusual is the characteristic that on Florida's west coast these shells are pink, while on the east coast the shells are yellowish. They are especially abundant in the Tampa Bay area.
Native from North Carolina to Florida and the West Indies.

Cockle and Clam

YELLOW EGGCOCKLE
Laevicardium mortoni
Also called LITTLE EGGCOCKLE or MORTON'S EGGCOCKLE.
Average size ¹/₂ inch, largest 1 inch; inedible.
White with tannish-brown markings, some zigzag lines,
circular lines and dots.
A glossy, ovate shell, moderately inflated and fairly thin.
The inside is white and polished, with the color markings
showing through.
A common shallow-water species. Wild ducks like to feed on them.
Native from Cape Cod, Massachusetts to Florida and the Gulf of Mexico.

SPINY PAPERCOCKLE
Papyridea lata
Average size 1 inch, largest 1¹/₂ inches;
inedible.
Outside white or cream, with rose,
orange and yellow flecks or mottlings.
Interior glossy, with violet and white col-
ors showing through, or sometimes
orange and brown.
Shell moderately fragile; ribs are inconspicuous in the center of the valves, but
are raised near the ends.
Moderately common from low tide to several fathoms.
Native from North Carolina to Florida, West Indies and the Gulf of Mexico.

SOUTHERN QUAHOG
Mercenaria campechiensis
Average size 2 inches, largest 5 inches; edible.
Interior white; outside dirty white.
A heavy shell, obese; sculpture of numerous,
concentric lines of growth. Interior is smooth
and glossy. Lunule heart-shaped. Inner margin
crenulate.

The Northern Quahog is used commercially
for chowders and as clams-on-the-half-shell or
"Cherrystones," while the Southern Quahog is common, but has not been exploit-
ed commercially to a great extent.
Found in bays in shallow water.
Native from Chesapeake Bay to Florida, Texas and Cuba.

Venus Clam

CROSS-BARRED VENUS
Chione cancellata

Average size ¹/₂ inch to 1 inch, largest ³/₄ inch; edible.
Outside is white, gray or buff; a brown color phase is found on the east coast of Florida. Lining usually glossy white with purple, though it may be deep orange.

There are narrow ridges across the surface of the valves, making a cross-barred pattern. Shape is roughly triangular.

Found in shallow water.

Native from North Carolina to Florida, Texas and the West Indies.

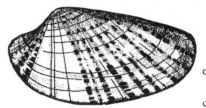

SUNRAY VENUS
Macrocallista nimbosa

Also called GIANT CALLISTA.

Average size 3 inches, largest 5 inches; edible.

Violet-gray with darker rays; slightly curved streaks radiate out from the hinge in a darker color. Interior dull white, with a tinge of red over central area. Fresh specimens are salmon-pink. Glossy.

A longish, clam-type shell with glossy, a smooth surface. An exceptionally pretty shell.

Found and gathered in large numbers on the shelling coasts. Used for ashtrays and often as unusual dishes. Native Americans used them as eating utensils.

Native to the Florida's west coast from St. Petersburg to Marco Island. On the east coast, as far north as North Carolina.

POINTED VENUS
Anomalocardia auberiana

Average size ¹/₂ inch, largest ³/₄ inch; inedible.
Creamy-white, white, tan with brown or purple specklings. Inside white, purple or brown.

Sharp, wedge-like rostrum at the posterior end. Shell is light in weight, with a tiny beak. Small, concentric ribs are more prominent near the beak. Lunule oval.

Found on sandy shores. Brackish-water specimens are dwarfed.

Native from North Carolina to Florida to Texas.

Clam and Tellin

CALICO CLAM
Macrocallista maculata

Also called CHECKERBOARD CLAM, SPOTTED CLAM.
Average size 1½ inches, largest 2½ inches; edible.
Exterior cream, with checkerboard markings of
brownish-red; interior polished white with yellow
or faint lavender markings.

A moderately strong, ovate shell. Surface is porcellaneous, with very fine radial
lines. The Venus shells are named for the Goddess Venus and they are noted for
their graceful lines and beauty of color and sculpture. These shells are very popular
with collectors.

Found in shallow water where there is a sandy bottom. Single valves are common on the beach in various locations.

Native from North Carolina to Florida and the West Indies.

DISC DOSINIA
Dosinia discus

Average size 2 inches, largest 3 inches; edible.

Pure white, both inside and outside, with a yellow periostracum.

Moderately thin; circular in outline; small but
prominent beak; compressed. Concentric ridges
number about 20 to 25 per inch. Another species
is Elegant Dosinia, which has about 50 concentric
ridges to the inch.

Gathered just offshore in moderately shallow water, with paired valves common
on southern beaches.

Native from Virginia to Florida, the Gulf States and the Bahamas.

SUNRISE TELLIN
Tellina radiata

Average size 2 inches, largest 4 inches; edible.

Polished white, with pale yellow or pink
from highest point to the margins. Interior all
white, with the external color showing through
in strong light. Beaks often red-tipped.

Elongated shell with striking coloring. Strong valves; often found with the two
halves still joined long after clam is dead.

Native from North Carolina to Florida and the Caribbean. More common in
the West Indies than in Florida.

Tellin

SPECKLED TELLIN
Tellina listeri
Also called INTERRUPTED TELLIN.
Average size 1 inch, largest 2
inches; inedible.

Creamy-white, with
purplish-brown rays or specklings
on the exterior. The interior is white with
the color showing through. The shell is moderately
thin, long, flattened, and not polished. The anterior is rounded and the posterior
end is twisted. The surface is sculptured with strong concentric lines.

Found in moderately shallow water, but buries itself deeper in the mud or sand
than most bivalves.

Native from North Carolina to Brazil.

ALTERNATE TELLIN
Tellina alternata
Also called LINED TELLIN.

Average size 2 inches, largest 3 inches;
edible.

Exterior white, flushed with yellow or
pink; interior glossy pink or yellow. Shell
solid, elongated and compressed; moder-
ately pointed and slightly twisted posterior end; anterior end rounded.

Sculpture has numerous evenly spaced, fine, concentric grooves.

Found in shallow water. Common,
Native from North Carolina to Florida and the Gulf States.

ROSE PETAL TELLIN
Tellina lineata
Average size 1½ inches, largest 2½
inches; edible.

These tellins are found in two colors:
white or watermelon red.

A moderately solid shell, inflated
slightly, moderately elongate. The outside
of the shell at first seems opalescent and
smooth, but on closer inspection has fine, concentric grooves.

Found in shallow water in bays.

Native to all Florida coasts and the West Indies.

Tellin and Semele

WHITE-CREST TELLIN
Tellidora cristata
Also called PANDORA'S BOX.
Average size 1 inch, largest 1½ inches; edible.
White in color.

Triangular-shaped, with one flat valve and the
other somewhat inflated. Margins at the back of
valves are saw-toothed. Faint concentric ridges on surface.
Found in mud or sand, close to shore.
Native from North Carolina to the west coast of Florida and Texas.

ATLANTIC SEMELE
Semele proficua
Also called FLORIDA SEMELE.
Average size 1 inch, largest 1½ inches; inedible.
Exterior white or yellowish-white; interior white
or yellowish. Florida specimens commonly have a
speckling of pink or purple.
Shell is thin and compressed, oval, with beaks
almost central. The sculpture has fine concentric lines. Interior is glossy.
Found in shallow water, buried in sandy mud.
Native from North Carolina to Florida and the West Indies.

PURPLISH SEMELE
Semele purpurascens
Average size 1 inch, largest 1½ inches; inedible.
White, gray or cream, with purple splotches or
zigzag lines on the outside. On the inside, white
blotched with purple or orange. Some specimens are
yellow instead of white.

Shell oval, with both ends rounded. Posterior end twice the
length of the anterior. Thin-shelled and smooth, except for very
fine, concentric growth lines.
Found in shallow water.
Native from North Carolina to Florida and the West Indies.

Coquina, Asaphis and Razor

VARIABLE COQUINA
Donax variabilis

Also called VARIABLE WEDGE SHELL and BUTTERFLY SHELL.
Average size ½ inch, largest ¾ inch; edible.

Found in all colors of the rainbow. The colors come in
solids of yellow-brown, blue, lavender, green, pink and varia-
tions. Many appear to have a plaid design.

This little clam creates the activity you see at the tide line
of the surf, on the gulf and the Atlantic ocean. With the aid of a "foot" which
darts out from one end, they can emerge or dig themselves under in a twinkling,
as a wave rolls up and recedes. Apparently this is because they are extremely light-
sensitive; they rush to get back into the darkness of the sand.

Coquinas have countless uses. Washed and boiled they make a fine soup. Their
shape and diverse colors make them adaptable to use in many varieties of shellcraft.

Native to Gulf and Atlantic coasts, especially from Daytona Beach to Panama
City. Also found as far north as Virginia.

GAUDY ASAPHIS
Asaphis deflorata

Also called COCKLE CLAM.

Average size 2 inches, largest 3 inches;
edible.

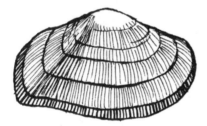

Pale yellow to orange on the outside.
Interior is of similar coloration, but more
intense. There is usually a deep purple
streak on the outer edge of the interior.

A strikingly-colored shell, unusually sculptured. Beaks are inflated and rolled
slightly in and under. Not plentiful in Florida waters, but occasionally taken.

Native to Southeast Florida, the Bahamas, West Indies

PURPLISH TAGELUS
Tagelus divisus

Average size 1 inch, largest 1½ inches;
edible.

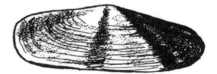

Whitish-purple in color, with a thin,
glossy brown outer skin. The shell is thin and elongated, with both ends rounded
bluntly.

Found in shallow water, they live in colonies buried in the sand.

Native from Cape Cod to south Florida, the Gulf States and the Caribbean.

Razor and Surfclams

GREEN JACKKNIFE CLAM
Solen viridis

Also called GREEN RAZOR CLAM or SHORT RAZOR CLAM.

Average size 2 inches, largest 4 inches; edible.

Pale green and white, with crescent-shaped brown marks across center of shell. Has greenish-brown skin. A thin, elongated shell with a nearly straight hinge line; the valves open at each end. There are very faint concentric wrinkles, but the surface is comparatively smooth.

Found on sand bars at low tide; also dredged in 25 fathoms. This razor clam lives in colonies and burrows into the sand vertically. Usually found in shallow bayous, where they burrow. Difficult to catch when danger threatens, because they can burrow as fast as you can dig.

Native from Rhode Island to northern Florida and the Gulf States.

FRAGILE SURFCLAM
Mactroma fragilis

Average size 2 inches, largest 2½ inches; edible.

Polished white, with a light brown or grayish skin in life.

Thin and elongated shell with sharp margins. Otherwise, it has the distinctive characteristics of the Surf Clam family. Found in shallow water, mostly around entrance to passes from ocean to inland waters.

Native from North Carolina to Florida to Texas, Mexico and the West Indies.

SOUTHERN SURFCLAM
Spisula solidissima similis

Average 4–5 inches, largest 7 inches; edible.

Color is yellowish-white, with a thin, yellowish-brown outer skin.

Strong and oval, rather smooth with small, irregular growth lines. Beaks are central and large; hinge is strong, with a spoon-shaped cavity inside. This is the largest bivalve on our Atlantic coast. Has a powerful foot which enables it to escape from its enemies. Gathered for food, it is popular for clam bakes.

Found below the low water mark on ocean beaches. Clammers drag the bottom with sharp sticks, and if one passes between open valves, the clam closes upon it and is drawn to the surface. Often washed up on the beach in great numbers after severe winter storms.

Native from Nova Scotia to South Carolina. Sub-species *S. solidissima similis* is more elongate and is found from Cape Cod to Florida and Texas.

Clam and Borer

CHANNELED DUCKCLAM
Raeta plicatella
Also called SAILOR'S EAR.
Average size 2 inches, largest 3 inches; edible.
Pure white interior and exterior.
Eggshell thin, but moderately strong.
Sculpture of concentric smooth, distinct ribs
which on the inside of the shell show as
grooves. Posterior end slightly gaping, anterior
end rounded; inflated.

Anatina anatina, or Smooth Duck Clam, has about the same shape as the
Sailor's Ear, but is moderately smooth except for irregular growth lines and tiny,
but distinct, concentric ribs near the beaks; uncommon.
Found washed ashore, but rarely seen alive.
Native from North Carolina to Florida to Texas and West Indies.

CONSTRICTED MACOMA
Macoma constricta
Average size 1 inch, largest 2¹/₂ inches; edible.
A white shell with a thin yellow or gray skin.
The back end is rather squared off and
notched below, and there is a slight fold from
the beaks to the margin. The other margins are
broadly rounded. Concentric growth lines are
stained the color of the skin.
Lives in moderately deep water.
Native along the Atlantic Coast from Florida to Texas and the West Indies.

ATLANTIC MUD-PIDDOCK
Barnea truncata
Also called FALLEN ANGELWING, TRUNCATED
BORER.

Average size 2 inches, largest 2¹/₂ inches; edible.
White to grayish-white.
A fragile shell. Rather oblong, with the back end cut off and broad at the tip.
This half is smooth. There are sharp scales at the front end. The siphon is encased
in a tubelike sheath and is 2 or 3 times the length of the shell.
This shell burrows into mud or peat, and is exposed at low tide. Because they
are very delicate, it is difficult to dig them out without crushing them.
Native from Massachusetts Bay to south Florida.

Angelwing and Piddock

ANGELWING
Cyrtopleura costata
Average size 4 inches, largest 8 inches; edible.

White, with indistinct markings, occasionally an irregular band of pink near the ventral margin. Has a thin gray skin in life.

Shaped something like a supposed "angel's wing," long and narrow, it is quite fragile, with about 30 beaded radial ribs. The strong radial sculpture extends the entire length of the shell.

These are most often found burrowed under the surface in shallow water, particularly in muddy spots, from three inches to three feet down. A colony of several usually will be found together. Latin people consider them quite tasty.

Native to all shores on the Gulf of Mexico and from Massachusetts to the West Indies.

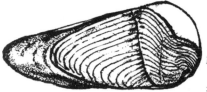

STRIATE PIDDOCK
Martesia striata
Also called WOOD PIDDOCK, STRIATED MARTESIA.

Average size ³/₄ inch, largest 1¹/₄ inches; inedible.

Grayish-white in color.

Wedge shaped, the back end gaping; front margin nearly closed. Elevated, scalloped lines mark the surface. Back end tapers with nearly straight edges, to a rounded tip.

This wood-boring clam is found on floating timbers or driftwood.

Native from West Florida to Texas and the West Indies.

RAM'S HORN SQUID
Spirula spirula
Average size 1 inch, largest 1¹/₂ inches; edible.

White interior and exterior.

This shell comes from the tail of a certain kind of squid. It is a chambered cone, coiled in a flat spiral.

Each chamber is separated by a septum, or wall, that is nacreous, white and fragile. Although these shells are found cast up on the beach, the animal lives in deep water.

Found worldwide.

Other Sea Life

LINED SEAHORSE
Hippocampus erectus

Average size 3 inches, largest on record 12 inches; edible.

Dusky, with pale grayish blotches, edged sharply with lighter and darker shades. Some of these are between the eyes and the neck.

The head and neck are arched somewhat like a horse's. The body is encased in bony rings and the tail is slender and tapering. The seahorse swims in an upright position and uses its tail to cling to seaweed or grass. The tail may be coiled when not in use. It has a tiny mouth at the end of the snout, through which it sucks its food. One of the plate-fish.

The male seahorse has a pouch in which the female deposits the eggs; here they remain until hatched.

Intensely interesting as specimens for saltwater aquariums.

They have been used for jewelry and decorative purposes, but they are increasingly rare and should not be harvested. In some South American countries they are considered a table delicacy.

Native to Florida, South America, and Pacific coasts.

SHORT-SPINED SEA URCHIN
Lytechinus variegatus

Average size 2 inches, largest 3½ inches; edible.

Spines are purple in this species, although other species of Sea Urchins are green and some are red. Sea urchins populate the waters of all oceans. They resemble a tennis ball covered with spines that can assume a waving motion.

Sea Urchin eggs feed many other creatures. A female will produce and discharge in the water over 20 million eggs a year. Only a microscopic portion develop, the rest are eaten by sea life. The male discharges an equal abundance of matter into the water, which is white in color, as contrasted to the female's deep orange-colored eggs. The sex products come from five large gonads in the upper part of the body cavity. In many parts of the world natives eat these, either raw or cooked. Some eat them on the spot, inserting a finger into the cavity, bring out the gonads, and devour them, unwashed.

Native to all oceans.

Other Sea Life

FIVE-SLOTTED SAND DOLLAR
Mellita quinquiesperforata

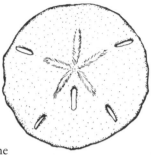

Also called KEYHOLE URCHIN.
Average size 3 inches, largest 5 inches; inedible.
Dark purplish-brown; turns green when taken from
water, and dead shells bleach to a dull white. The flat,
thin shell has five slits which resemble keyholes. It is
covered above and below with minute, velvety spines. A
delicate design, like the petals of a flower, is etched on the
under surface—from this, tube feet protrude, enabling the animal to breathe and to
move about. The spines also aid movement. The sand dollar does not seem able to
right itself if turned on its rounded side. The mouth is centered on the underside.

Found in lagoons or sandy beaches. Native to Florida and the West Indies.

ATLANTIC HORSESHOE CRAB
Limulus polyphemus

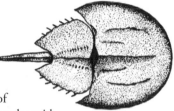

Average size 6 inches, largest 14 inches
(one authority claims 20); inedible.
Light buff or brown. There are two large
compound eyes rather far apart on the upper side of
the shell and two small simple eyes close together on the mid-
dle line, near the front border. Below the upper shell is the abdomen, with six pairs
of spines. Plate like appendages on the abdomen act as breathing organs, though
the first pair, overlapping, act as a cover. There are five pairs of legs ending in pin-
cers, and one pair with narrow plates that form a cone which helps the crab push
its way through sand and mud. Horseshoe Crabs come ashore in huge groups and
lay an enormous number of eggs in the sand near the shoreline. These eggs are an
important food source for migrating birds.

Native from Nova Scotia to Florida.

COMMON STARFISH
Echinaster sentus

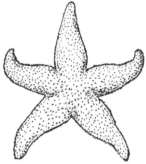

Also known as COMMON SEASTAR.
Average size 3 inches, largest 7 inches; inedible.
Starfish belong to the Phylum Enchinoderma. All are
five-pointed, or pentagonal, and have five arms as a mini-
mum, sometimes more. Spines cover the body in a mosaic
pattern on top. Starfish have no heads, but instead have
tiny eyes at the ends of the arms, and can lead with any of them, in movement.
They are able to grow a new am if one is knocked off.

Found on intertidal sand flats. Found in all oceans.

Other Sea Life

CORAL! Who has not heard the word and been fascinated by it and wondered how it grows in the many sizes and shapes? Coral is a limestone formation in the sea which is produced by the activity of billions of tiny, jelly-like animals. The coral-forming animals are known as "polyps," from the Greek words meaning "many feet." They are sac-like in form. The mouth is at the upper end, surrounded by arms or tentacles. Coral polyps can absorb the calcium that is dissolved in seawater and deposit it beneath and around their bodies, to form a cup or "calyx" of limestone.

STAGHORN CORAL   FINGER CORAL

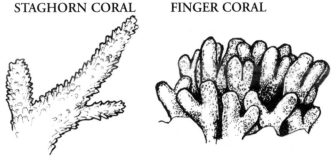

Acropora cervicornis   *Porites porites*

Coral polyps reproduce by means of eggs and also by budding. In this way they grow off other individuals, like themselves, just as branches grow to form a tree. The polyps remain close to each other and thus form colonies. The combined limestone-forming activity of these colonies often produces a coral mass of a large size. These may take the shape of small irregular crusts, large dome-shaped masses, or tree-like, branched structures, varying from small clusters to huge, towering growths.

BRAIN CORAL   PURPLE SEAFAN

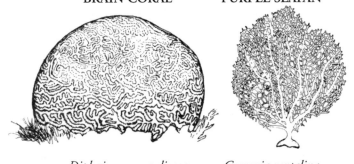

Diplori   *a clivosa*   *Gorgonia ventalina*

The living polyps cover the outside of these masses and are responsible for the beautiful colors of the coral reef, ranging from shades of tan, brown, orange and yellow, through pink, rose, purple, and green. When the coral is removed from the water, the polyps die and, if washed off, leave behind the snowy white limestone "skeleton." The Gorgonias are in the Coral family.

There are no coral reefs on the East American coast north of Florida and Bermuda. Small patches of a species of coral are found as far north as New England, and some growths of certain coral even extend to the Arctic Circle. In the deep sea, small specialized coral species are also found. The reef-forming coral polyps will not live in waters colder than 65 degrees Fahrenheit.

INDEX

*Color plates numbers are given in bold type.

PLATE 1

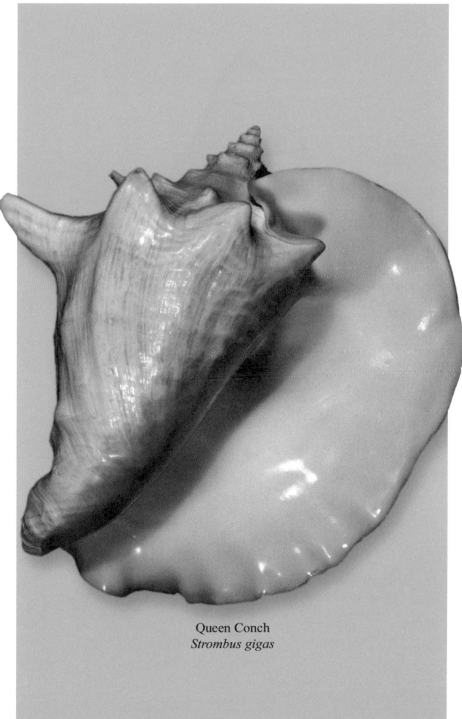

Queen Conch
Strombus gigas

PLATE 2

Eastern Banded Tulip
Fasciolaria hunteria

Leafy Jewelbox
Chama macerophylla

PLATE 3

American Horsemussel
Modiolus americanus

Ponderous Ark
Noetica ponderosa

Mossy Ark
Arca imbricata

PLATE 4

White Baby Ear
Sinum perspectivum

Cross-Barred Venus
Chione cancellata

Florida Lucine
Pseudomiltha floridana

Buttercup Lucine
Anodontia alba

Pennsylvania Lucine
Lucina pennsylvanica

Broad-Ribbed Carditid
Carditamera floridana

Florida Spiny Jewelbox
Arcinella corunata

Spiny Papercockle
Papyridea lata

PLATE 5

Gaudy Asaphis (yellow and orange)
Asaphis deflorata

Variable Coquinas
Donax variabilis

Rose Petal Tellin
Tellina lineata

Alternate Tellin
Tellina alternata

PLATE 6

Atlantic Kittenpaw
Plicatula gibbosa

Frond Oyster
Lopha frons

Atlantic Calico Scallop
Argopecten gibbus

Ornate Scallop
Chlamys ornata

Lettered Olive
Oliva sayana

Bay Scallop
Argopecten irradians concentricus

PLATE 7

Common Nutmeg
Cancellaria reticulata

Lion's Paw
Lyropecten nodosus

Atlantic Wing-oyster
Pteria colymbus

Female   Male

PLATE 8

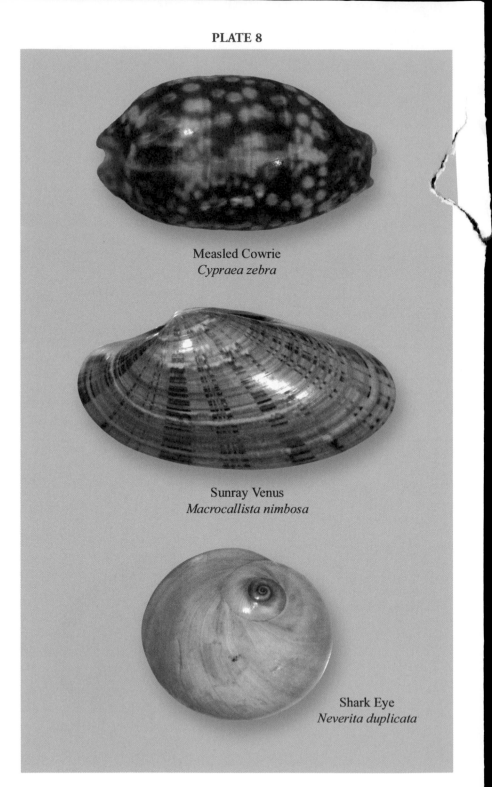

Measled Cowrie
Cypraea zebra

Sunray Venus
Macrocallista nimbosa

Shark Eye
Neverita duplicata

PLATE 9

Scotch Bonnets
Semicassis granulata granulata

Apple Murex
Chicoreus pomum

Lace Murex
Chicoreus florifer dilectus

PLATE 10

Sundial Shell
Architectonica nobilis

Fargo's Wormsnail
Vermicularia fargoi

Florida Wormsnail
Vermicularia knorri

Fragile Surfclam
Mactrotoma fragilis

Southern Surfclam
Spisula solidissima similis

PLATE 11

Crown Conch
Melongena corona

Lightning Whelk
Busycon sinistrum

PLATE 12

Eastern Oyster
Crassotrea virginica

Dwarf Tiger Lucine
Codakia orbiculata

Southern Quahog
Mercenaria campechiensis

PLATE 13

Atlantic Pearl-oyster
Pinctada imbricata

Sawtooth Pen Shell
Atrina serrata

Stiff Pen Shell
Atrina rigida

PLATE 14

Cayenne Keyhole Limpet
Diodora cayensis

Florida Top Shell
Calliostoma euglyptum

Knobby Top
Turbo castanea

Purplish Semele
Semele purpurascens

White-Crest Tellin
Tellidora cristata

Atlantic Semele
Semele proficua

PLATE 15

Crown Cone
Conus regius

Dislocated Auger
Terebra disloca

Common West Indian Bubble
Bulla striata

Turkey Wing
Arca zebra

Transverse Ark
Anadara transversa

PLATE 16

Sunrise Tellin
Tellina radiata

Disc Dosinia
Dosinia discus

Calico Clam
Macrocallista maculata